LASERS

To my sons Jeff and Jeremy

Library of Congress Number: 80-17871

1 2 3 4 5 6 7 8 9 0 84 83 82 81

Printed and bound in the United States of America.

Library of Congress Cataloging in Publication Data

Johnson, Jim, 1943-
    Lasers.

    (A Look inside)
    Includes index.
    SUMMARY: Discusses the development of the first
modern laser, the parts of a laser and how they work,
and applications of lasers in medicine and technology.
    1. Lasers — Juvenile literature. [1. Lasers]
I. Mille, Mark. II. Blair, Jay. III. Title.
IV. Series: Look inside.
TA1682.J64   621.36'6   80-17871
ISBN 0-8172-1400-3

LASERS

By James Johnson

Illustrated by Jay Blair and Mark Mille
Cover illustration by Mark Mille

CONTENTS

RAINTREE PUBLISHERS
Milwaukee • Toronto • Melbourne • London

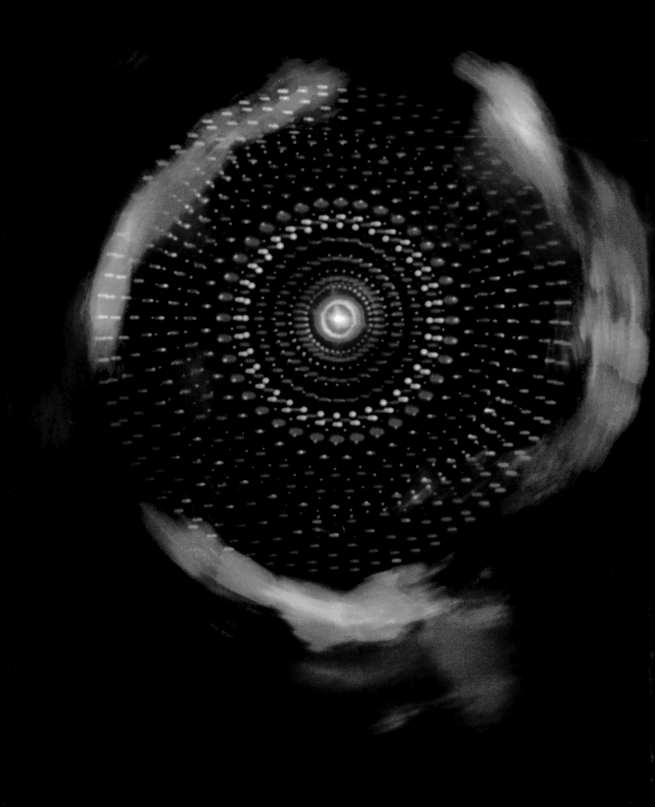

LASER LIGHT

Light is very important to us. The early cave people depended on the light and heat made by a fire to see at night and to warm their surroundings. As people learned more about science, they learned new ways to make light. The light bulb invented by Thomas Edison was a tremendous improvement. The light bulb uses a small strand of wire heated by an electric current. When the wire gets hot enough, it glows and gives off light. People learned that certain types of gas such as helium, neon, and mercury vapor also give off light when electricity flows through them.

In 1960 Dr. Theodore Maiman made and used the first laser. Many types of lasers have been made since his first working model, but that laser started a search for new ways for light to help humanity.

A laser light show

Laser effects by LASERIUM

"normal" light is broken into a spectrum

The race to make the first laser started in 1957. In that year Dr. Charles Townes and Dr. A. L. Schawlow wrote an article explaining the theory of a laser. Even though Dr. Townes and Dr. Schawlow knew how the laser should work, they did not build one because just the right combination of materials had to be arranged in the right order. Three years passed before Dr. Maiman found the right combination and made his ruby laser.

Since its invention, the laser has been used in many different ways. Some of the uses have been removing the bristles from pigs' skin, operating on human eyes, drilling the holes in baby bottle nipples, welding and cutting metals, and measuring distances.

The beam of light that comes from a laser has more uses than the light from other light sources such as candles, light bulbs, and neon signs. That's because laser light is:

monochromatic light is only one color

1. monochromatic
2. directional
3. coherent
4. bright

Monochromatic means "one color." A laser produces light of only one color. "Normal" light sources produce a wide range of colors.

A spectrum is a record of the colors produced by a light source. To make a spectrum, shine a thin beam of light at a prism. The prism is a piece of glass in the shape of a triangle.

Each color of light going through a prism is bent by the glass in a slightly different direction. When the white light from an ordinary light bulb goes through a prism, a spectrum comes out. White light is therefore made up of all the colors that our eyes can see, from red on one end of the spectrum to blue on the other end.

If laser light is put through a prism, it is bent, but it is not separated into different colors. This tells us that a laser produces only one color of light.

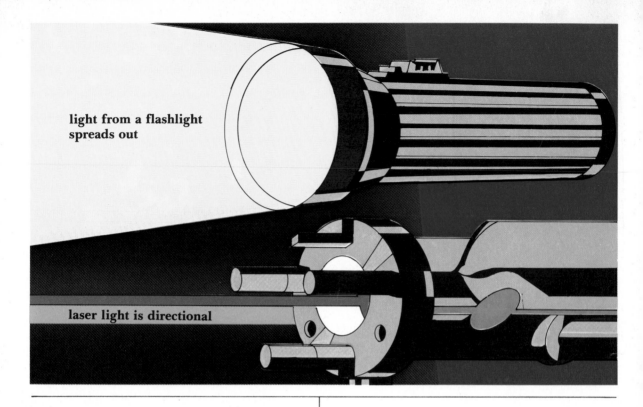

light from a flashlight spreads out

laser light is directional

The second reason that laser light is different from ordinary light is that laser light is *directional*. It simply does not spread out as much as ordinary light. A common laboratory laser may spread so its beam covers about .3 meters (1 foot) at a distance of 305 meters (1,000 feet) from the laser. In comparison a flashlight would cover about a 61 meter (200 foot) circle at the same distance.

If the laser beam is sent through a special telescope called a collimator it will spread out even less. Laser beams have been sent enormous distances through space and the beam has remained narrow enough to be useful. For instance, a laser beam has been used to measure the distance to the moon. The beam travels 402,000 kilometers (250,000 miles) from the earth to the moon and has only spread to cover about a 3 kilometer (2 mile) circle on the moon's surface. No ordinary light is directional enough to do that.

The third thing that makes laser light different is *coherence*. To understand coherence we must think of light as being a wave, like a wave in a pond.

All waves of light coming from a laser are in phase, or in step, with each other. This means that all the waves start at the same moment and are the same size. Ordinary light sources produce waves that are not in step with each other. Coherent light could be compared to a group of soldiers marching in step with each other. Incoherent light would be like people walking down a crowded sidewalk in a large city. Each line of soldiers steps together, moving in exactly the same direction and arriving at a certain place at the same time. Marching is a good way to move a lot of people in an orderly manner. In the same way, coherent waves work well in moving a large amount of energy. This is the property of laser light that allows us to make three dimensional pictures called holograms. We'll talk about holograms later.

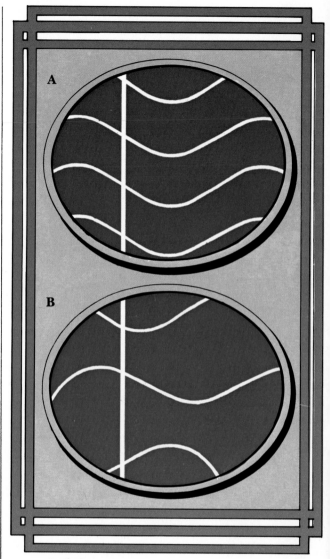

A. Coherent light

B. Incoherent light

brightness of normal light

The fourth special property of laser light is *brightness*. All light waves in a laser beam work together. They spread out very little as they travel and they are all of the same color. There is more energy within the beam from a laser than there is in the same size beam from any other light source, even the sun. A 40 watt light bulb hardly gives enough light to read this book, but a 40 watt laser can be used to melt metals. A 3 watt light bulb is not large enough to be a good night-light, but a 3 watt laser can easily burn wood. Laser light is the brightest light we know.

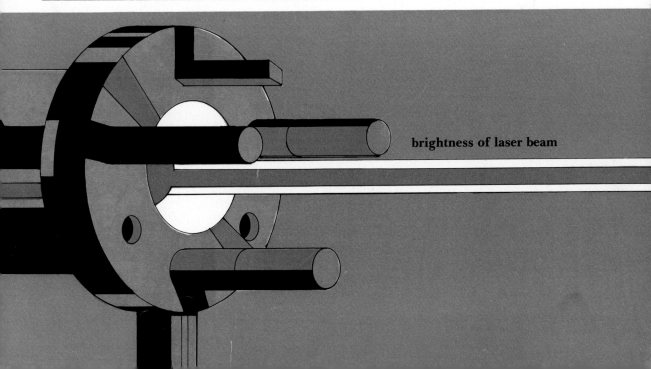

brightness of laser beam

THE PARTS OF A LASER

Lasers range in size from a few millimeters in diameter to those that need a 12-story building to hold a single laser. The light power they produce varies also from less than 1/1000 watt to several hundred million watts. Even though lasers vary greatly in size and output, they all have the same four working parts.

The four parts to all lasers are:
1. the excitation mechanism
2. the active medium
3. the feedback mechanism
4. the output coupler

An argon laser beam is split by a prism. Two mirrors direct the beam back to a central point.

The Aerospace Corporation

13

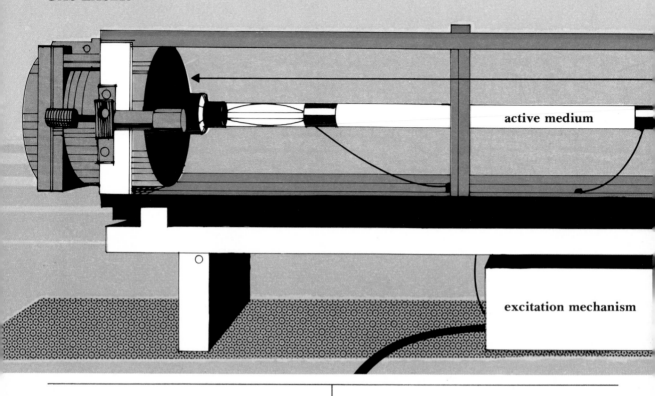

active medium

excitation mechanism

All lasers need something to give them energy. This is called the *excitation mechanism*. After the energy is in the laser, there must be a part where the energy becomes laser light and is amplified (made stronger). This part is called the *active medium* because it is the part that actually makes the laser light. A mirror is placed at each end of the active medium. When light from the active medium strikes this mirror, it bounces back to the active medium to be amplified further. The system of mirrors is called the *feedback mechanism* because they feed the light back into the active medium. One of the mirrors is specially made to allow some of the light to escape the active medium. The amount of light that escapes is the laser output beam. The special mirror is called the *output coupler*.

Common excitation mechanisms (which give energy to the laser) are either optical

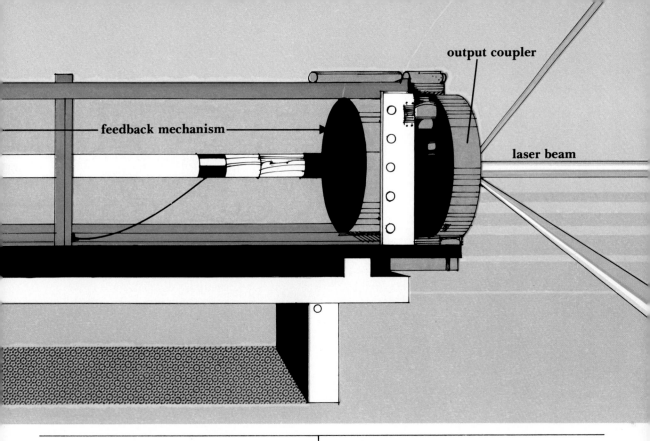

feedback mechanism

output coupler

laser beam

or electrical. The choice of excitation mechanism depends upon the type of active medium used. When a gas is the active medium, electrical excitation is used most often. Powerful electricity is applied directly to the gas, which takes in the energy and turns it into light. The active mediums of solid lasers use optical excitation mechanisms. Electricity lights up special, very bright lamps which are placed near the solid active medium. The light energy from these intense lamps is stored by the active medium and turned into laser light.

Active mediums (where energy becomes laser light) may be either solids, liquids, gases, or semi-conductor crystals. The active medium should be thought of as being the part of the laser that stores the energy coming from the excitation mechanism. The active medium then converts the energy into laser light.

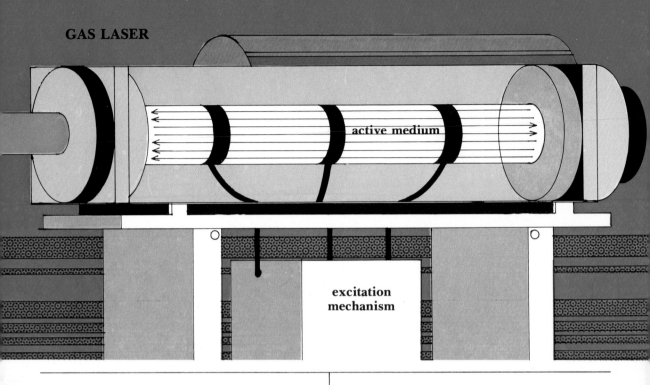

GAS LASER

active medium

excitation
mechanism

Lasers are sometimes named according to their active medium. For example, a ruby laser uses a piece of solid crystal ruby for the active medium. This ruby is made in the shape of a rod. The size of the rod may vary from being a few millimeters wide and a few centimeters long to about 2 centimeters (.8 inch) wide and 35 centimeters (14 inches) long. Within limits, the larger the piece of ruby, the more powerful will be its laser beam.

Gas lasers use a gas or a mixture of gases for the active medium. The helium-neon (HeNe) gas laser is a common example of a laser that uses a mixture of two gases for an active medium. Some liquids are also used for active mediums, although these lasers are not as common as gas or solid lasers. Small electronic devices using crystals are also used for active mediums. These are called diode lasers or semi-conductor lasers. They are very small but are being used more each day.

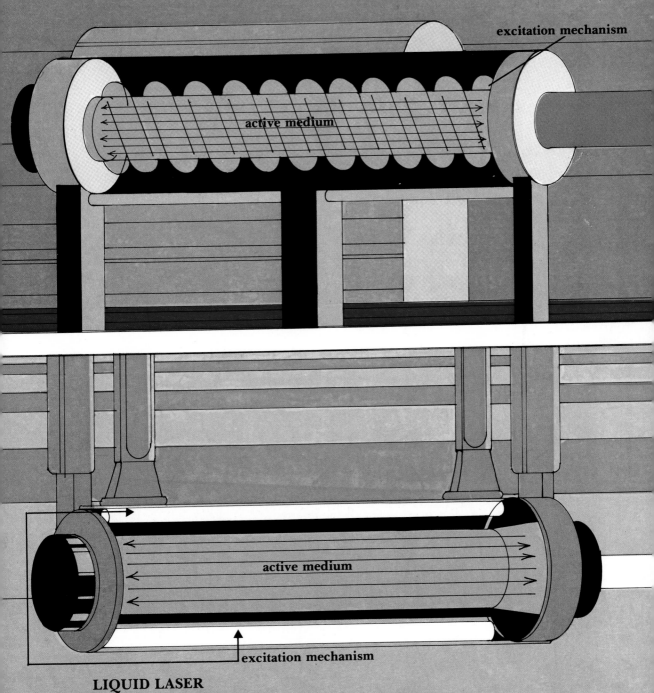

SOLID LASER

excitation mechanism

active medium

active medium

excitation mechanism

LIQUID LASER

The laser light that is produced inside the active medium is at first very weak. Its power must be increased or amplified before it is very useful. The light can be amplified by making it stay inside the excited active medium longer. A mirror is placed at the end of the active medium to return the small amount of laser light back into the active medium to be amplified further. When the light reaches the other end of the active medium, another mirror returns a large amount of the light again to be amplified. The light bounces back and forth between the two mirrors and gains energy from the active medium. By doing this the light is greatly amplified.

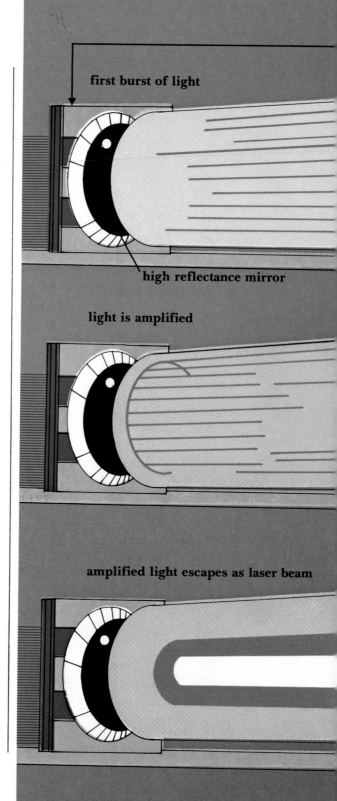

first burst of light

high reflectance mirror

light is amplified

amplified light escapes as laser beam

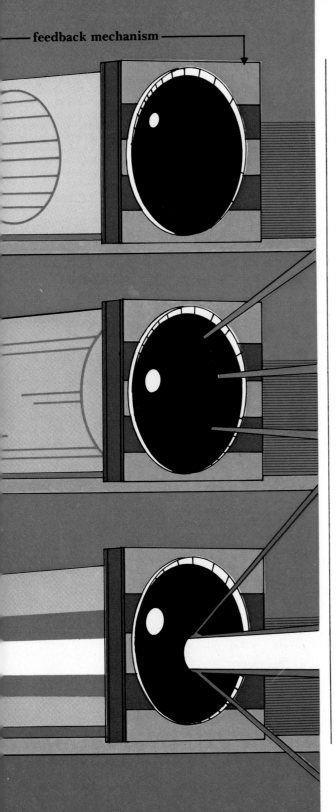

feedback mechanism

The mirrors are called the feedback mechanism (because they feed light back into the active medium). They must be placed very carefully for the light to bounce between them without being lost. They are specially made too. Ordinary mirrors will not work because they do not reflect enough of the light that hits them. Mirrors used in lasers must reflect almost 100% of the light striking them. Ordinary mirrors reflect only about 80%.

The two laser mirrors are not exactly the same. One of them is called the H.R. mirror, which stands for High Reflectance. This mirror is designed to reflect nearly 100% of the laser light striking it. The second mirror allows some of the light to reflect but lets the rest of the light go right through. This mirror is called the output coupler because it allows some of the laser light to get out.

LASER ACTION

Step 1

The excitation mechanism pumps energy into the active medium.

Step 2

The active medium stores the energy for a short time. It releases a small burst of light.

Step 3

The light picks up more energy from the active medium.

Step 4

The light bounces off the special mirror. It returns to the active medium to be amplified more.

Step 5

The amplified light beam hits the output coupler.

Step 6

Some of the amplified light is released by the output coupler. This is the laser beam. The rest of the light bounces back to the active medium to be amplified some more.

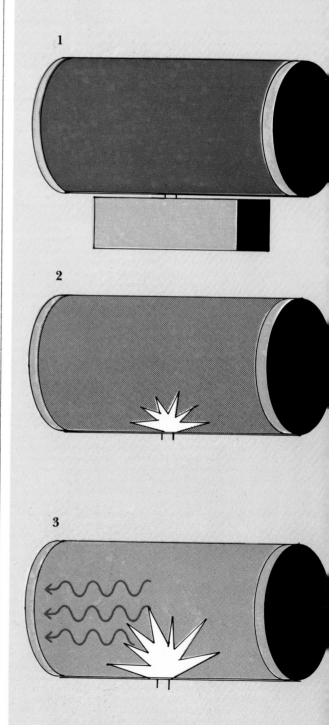

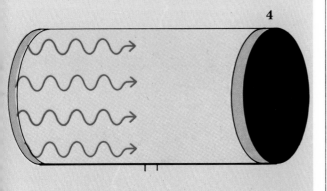

4

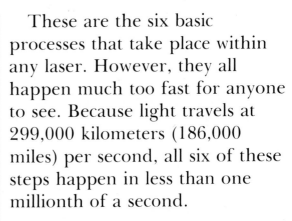

These are the six basic processes that take place within any laser. However, they all happen much too fast for anyone to see. Because light travels at 299,000 kilometers (186,000 miles) per second, all six of these steps happen in less than one millionth of a second.

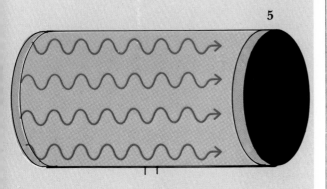

5

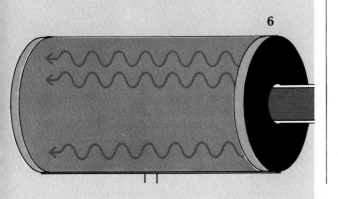

6

LASER BEAMS

Many different types of lasers have been used for different purposes. Each type of laser has an output beam which is different from other types of lasers. The kind of the output beam decides which laser will be used for a given job.

Some lasers produce a beam which is on continuously (all the time). These are called C.W. lasers (the C.W. stands for Continuous Wave). Other lasers can only give a short pulse of light.

The energy produced by a pulsed laser is measured in a unit called joules. One joule is the amount of light energy produced by a one-watt light bulb when it is on for one second. Pulsed lasers have been built to produce bursts of energy from a few thousandths of a joule to over 100 joules. The speed with which a laser delivers its energy is very important. If a pulsed laser produced one joule of energy in a burst that lasted 100 seconds, only 1 joule/100 sec or 1/100 of a

An argon laser heats metal

Coherent, Palo Alto, California

23

watt of power would reach the target. But if the same laser delivered one joule of energy in 1/1000 second then

$$\frac{1 \text{ joule}}{1/1000 \text{ sec}}$$

or 1000 watts of power are delivered. A one-joule ruby laser producing a light pulse lasting for 1/1000 second will drill a clean hole in a razor blade.

If the pulse were even shorter, for example 1/1,000,000 second, but the energy was still one joule, the power produced would be

$$\frac{1 \text{ joule}}{1/1,000,000 \text{ secs}}$$

or 1,000,000 watts.

Along with energy and pulse time, another important measurement of a laser beam is its "power density." This is a measurement of the concentration of the laser energy. (Something is concentrated when it is held together tightly.)

CO_2 laser cutting through steel

24

Spectra-Physics

Certainly one watt of power spread over this entire page will do less damage than will one watt concentrated into a spot the size of the period at the end of the sentence. Power density is measured in watts per square centimeter, written like this: watts/cm².

When lasers are used on a job the beam must often be focused to get the proper size and power density. A lens is used to focus a laser beam in much the same way a person can use a lens to concentrate sunlight for starting a campfire.

The laser output beam can be closely controlled. The excitation mechanism can be set to give the exact power and beam concentration for a particular job. This controls the amount of energy fed into the active medium and will therefore also control the laser power output. The laser beam is also controlled by choosing the proper lens to concentrate or spread the beam.

USING LASERS

People have used the laser for thousands of reasons since its invention in 1960. Some of these applications have been very successful. For a laser to be used permanently on any job, it must do the job better than an old method, or do the job at a lower cost. The list of uses here is not complete, but it shows some of the best ways lasers have been used.

A dye laser used in research.

Coherent, Palo Alto, California

A check-out counter with a built-in laser "reads" a UPC.

Universal Product Code

The low power HeNe laser is by far the most common laser made. It is being built into an automatic check-out counter used in supermarkets. Nearly every product bought today has a printed code on it. The code is called the Universal Product Code and is made of a series of varying sized lines. The size and space between these lines make up a code which identifies the product it appears on. The

A video disk player

product is passed over a window in the check-out station. A HeNe laser beam is reflected from the code and received by a sensitive detector. A computer then tells the cash register to print the name of the product and its cost for the customer to see. This laser system reduces the chances of errors in checking out and labeling the products. It also makes it much easier for the store owner to keep records.

A HeNe laser is being built into video disk players, which carry programs for television sets. The laser beam picks up information from a specially made record, much the same way the sound is picked up from a regular phonograph record by the needle. The beam reflecting from the special disk is the signal needed to produce a picture on any ordinary television set.

The carbon dioxide laser is high-powered, and the fact that it can be either pulsed or continuous makes it very useful in industry. Its beam is invisible, but can be very intense.

A laser melts and cuts metal in the same way a torch does; by applying heat. The difference is that the laser applies the heat much faster and is concentrated. The metal melts and then vaporizes and is blown out of the area before the heat can be carried away. Laser cutting produces clean cuts and does not weaken the metal like torch cutting.

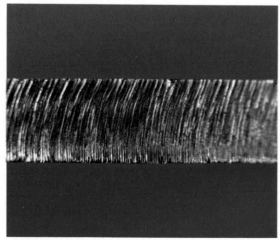

The edge of a piece of laser-cut steel

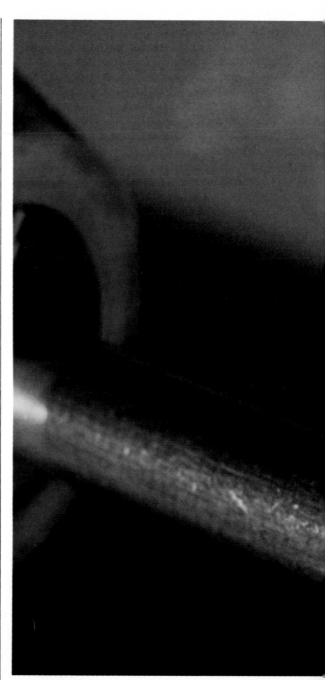

laser welding

Spectra-Physics

The laser is very good for welding small parts that must be done very accurately. Most laser metal cutters and welders are controlled with a computer and can make small welds in tiny parts that cannot be done with other welders. Experimental lasers producing 100,000 watts of continuous power have been used to weld steel as thick as 3.8 centimeters (1.5 inches). These lasers are not available to industries today, but lasers that produce 15,000 watts of continuous power are available. Steel as thick as 1 centimeter (.4 inches) can be cut and welded with these large carbon dioxide lasers.

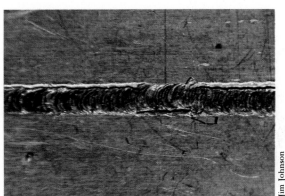

Jim Johnson

The seam where two pieces of metal have been laser-welded

31

The medical use of the laser is probably the best known. Today there are three major ways that lasers are used in medicine. These are in eye surgery, skin treatments, and as a cutting tool in surgery.

Certain types of eye diseases cause small blood vessels in the back of the eye to burst. This part of the eye is called the retina. The image formed by the eye appears on the retina, where nerves sense the image and send a signal to the brain. When blood vessels on the retina burst, the blood stops the light from going through the eye and therefore causes blindness. In the past very little could be done to prevent this type of blindness, but today a successful treatment using the laser is available. The beam from an argon laser is sent through the front portions of the eye and focused on the bleeding retinal vessel. In a fraction of a second,

Inner-ear surgery with an argon laser

Spectra-Physics

the intense laser light burns a small spot on the retina to stop the bleeding. The area on the retina where the beam strikes is damaged, but the injured area is so small that it does not affect the overall vision. The treatment is practically painless and takes only a few minutes.

Because the laser output can be accurately controlled, it is fast becoming accepted as a cutting tool in surgery. The laser cuts with an intense heat which seals the small blood vessels as it cuts. The loss of body fluids, such as blood, can be reduced greatly.

Much research is being done on the use of lasers in medicine. In the next few years many new and exciting uses of lasers in medicine are possible, including the treatment of some forms of cancer and arthritis.

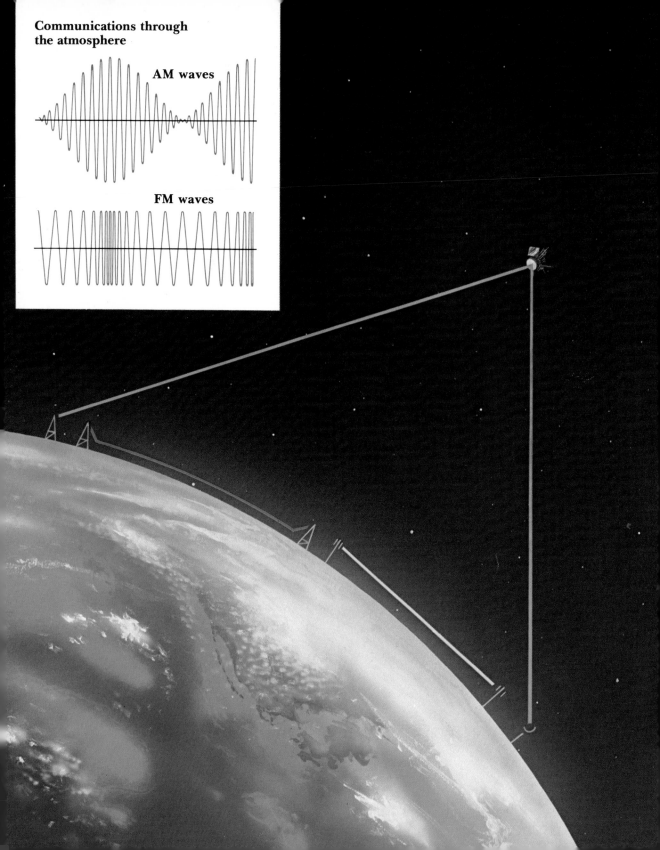

Communications through the atmosphere

AM waves

FM waves

Probably the greatest use of lasers in the future will be in the area of communications. Electromagnetic waves are used to carry information through the air in radio and TV. The number of times a wave repeats itself each second is called its frequency and is measured in hertz. One hertz is one wave per second. The amount of information sent by radio, television, or telephone signals depends upon the frequency of the signal. Standard A.M. radio operates at a few thousand hertz. More information (better quality music) is heard on F.M. radio where the frequency is increased to several million hertz. The frequency of light is about 100 million times greater than F.M. radio waves. It has been said that all the telephone communications for Chicago and New York City could be carried on a single cable little more than 2.5 centimeters (1 inch) wide if light were used rather than lower frequency waves.

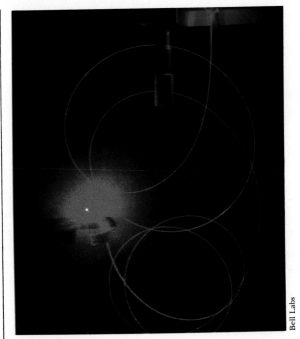

an optic fiber

Bell Labs

When a laser beam is sent through the air, it can be affected by rain, snow, fog, dust, or smoke. Special glass fiber optics have been developed to "pipe" light to desired places. Light sent through a fiber optic will stay inside the fiber even around corners or bends. These fibers are made with protective coatings and can be laid in underground pipes in the same way as telephone wires.

The military was the first large-scale user of lasers. Contrary to popular belief, the laser is not used as a ray gun. It is used to find out how far away an object is. An airplane or tank might have a laser range finder. It usually contains a Nd:YAG laser that sends out rapid pulses of invisible light to an object (maybe the target). The light pulses reflect from the object and return to the sender. A computer determines the distance to the target by measuring the time it took the pulses to make the round trip. These range finders measure distance very accurately.

The same procedure was used to measure the distance to the moon. Reflectors placed on the moon by astronauts were the target for pulses from a ruby laser. The time of the beam flight was recorded by very sensitive electronic circuits. The distance to the moon was measured to within a couple of meters.

military range finder

Hughes Aircraft Co.

part of a fusion laser

Many scientists believe that the laser will someday help to solve the energy crisis we are now facing. The laser is expected to be able to start a nuclear fusion reaction. This reaction is the same as the one taking place in the sun. It is the process where two hydrogen atoms are forced to unite with each other under extreme heat. When they are made to unite they produce a helium atom and enormous amounts of energy. The problem has been to produce the extreme heat necessary to start the reaction. It is expected that giant lasers can focus sufficient energy on a small target of hydrogen to raise the temperature high enough to start a fusion reaction. If lasers can start the reaction as predicted, enough energy will be available for all our electrical needs. Fusion is particularly desirable because there is a lot of hydrogen fuel in sea water, and enormous amounts of energy can come from a small amount of fuel. In addition, the dangerous radioactive waste made by present day nuclear reactors is not produced in the fusion reaction.

Laser fusion reactions seem possible and appear to have great advantages over present methods of producing electricity. However, it will take years of research and development before large amounts of electricity can be produced by fusion.

LASER ART

Holography is a fascinating form of photography that became possible with the invention of the laser. When coherent laser light reflects from an object and exposes photographic film, a record is produced on the film. The record looks like bent lines and does not look anything like the object itself. But when laser light is again sent through the film an exact image of the original object is produced. The image is produced behind the film and looks as though you were seeing it through a window.

Hologram art

© Rudie Berkhout

MAKING AND SHOWING
A HOLOGRAM

Holograms can be made by dividing the beam from a single laser into two beams which will be coherent and monochromatic. One of the beams is spread and sent directly to the film. This is called the reference beam. The other beam is spread and shines on the object we wish to photograph. We'll call this the "object beam." Light then reflects from the object to the film. At the film, the reflected object beam meets the reference beam. Where these two beams meet, they form an interference pattern. This pattern makes the bent light and dark lines on the film. After exposing the film, the interference pattern has been stored. It looks nothing like the

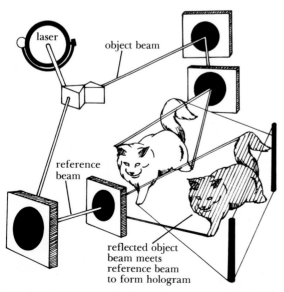

laser

object beam

reference beam

reflected object beam meets reference beam to form hologram

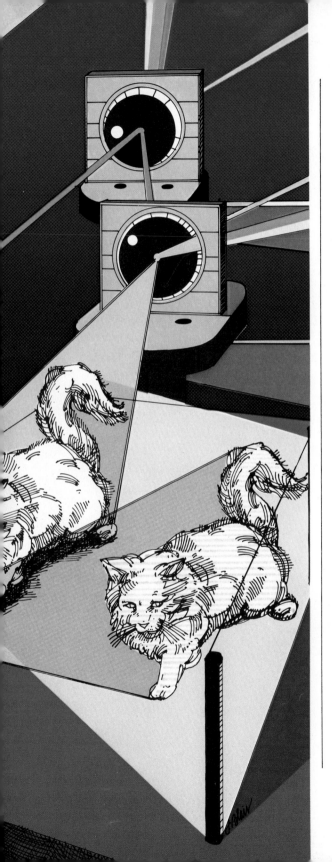

object, but it has recorded important information about the way that object reflects light.

After the film is developed, the hologram is viewed by shining the reference beam on the film. The light from the reference beam is broken up by the interference pattern on the film and some of the light is sent in the same directions as the previous object beam. When the viewer looks through the film into this reproduced object beam, he or she sees the object as it was when the film was exposed. The image that is seen looks like the original object in every way. It is the same size, it has the appearance of depth, and if done properly all sides of the object can be seen in the hologram.

Holography is an exciting new form of art and is being used for displaying products by some companies. True three-dimensional movies are thought possible using holography. Holograms can even be used in medicine and industry.

WORKING WITH LASERS

When people realize that lasers produce extremely powerful beams they are normally concerned about the dangers of working near lasers. Not all lasers are dangerous, but certainly there are lasers that must be used properly to prevent people from being injured. The government has grouped lasers into four classifications according to their potential hazard. Class I lasers are those which produce no known safety hazard. People could look directly into a Class I laser all day without any danger to their eyes. The supermarket check-out system and the video disk unit discussed earlier use Class I lasers.

Scientists at Bell Labs line up an optical fiber which makes up a one-kilometer long laser.

Bell Labs

Class II lasers are those that could cause damage to an eye if the person stared directly into the beam for a long time. A momentary flash of the light from a Class II laser will do no damage. Most HeNe lasers used in a classroom for demonstrations are Class II lasers. These lasers will have a yellow "CAUTION" sign on them telling you not to stare directly into the beam.

Class III lasers produce enough power to be dangerous to an eye. When a laser is directed into an eye the light is focused to a small spot on the retina. The power density in this spot may be high enough to cause damage to the retina. The damage could result in small blind spots in the person's vision. These lasers are labelled with a red and white "DANGER" sign warning people to avoid getting the direct beam into the eye.

Class IV lasers will produce

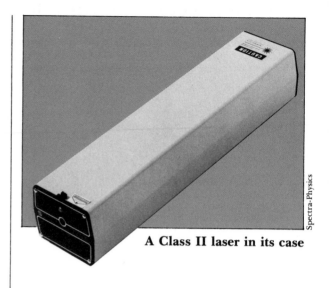

A Class II laser in its case

serious eye damage even from scattered reflections of the beam. These lasers will also produce serious skin burns if a person is exposed to the beam. The person operating a class IV laser must take precautions to avoid being hurt. He or she must use special glasses to protect the eyes and direct the beam to a safe target area. When Class IV lasers are used to cut or weld metals, or for other applications, they are

A Class IV ring dye laser with the cover off

This laser is operated with the cover off for illustration purposes only. The standard product has a BRH interlock which prevents lasing when the cover is removed.

Spectra-Physics

usually enclosed by a cabinet so that people cannot be exposed to the beam. When this is done the laser is safe to use without eye or skin protection.

The invention of the laser opened up new uses of light that were never dreamed of by the inventors of earlier light sources. Like all forms of technology, the laser can be used to benefit people by improving their living conditions, but when it is misused it can cause injury.

The number of lasers being used in medicine, research, and industry, communications, military and consumer products is growing very rapidly. This rapid growth makes it difficult for the laser industry to find enough people trained to work with laser equipment. The future holds challenging jobs as laser scientists, engineers or technicians for people who will enjoy exploring the many possibilities of laser light.

PRONUNCIATION GUIDE

These symbols have the same sound as the
darker letters in the sample words.

ə	balloon, ago
a	map, have
ä	father, car
b	ball, rib
d	did, add
e	bell, get
f	fan, soft
g	good, big
h	hurt, ahead
i	rip, ill
ī	side, sky
j	join, germ
k	king, ask
l	let, cool
m	man, same
n	no, turn
ō	cone, know
ȯ	all, saw
p	part, scrap
r	root, tire
s	so, press
sh	shoot, machine
t	to, stand
ü	pool, lose
u̇	put, book
v	view, give
w	wood, glowing
y	yes, year
′	strong accent
′	weak accent

46

GLOSSARY

These words are defined the way
they are used in the book.

active medium (ak′ tiv mēd′ ē
əm) the part of the laser that
changes energy into light and
then amplifies it.

amplify (am′ plə fī) to make
stronger.

coherent (kō hir′ ənt) moving
together at the same time.

collimator (käl′ ə mād ər) a
special telescope that helps
control the laser light.

continuous (kən tin′ yə wəs)
taking place all the time
without a break.

directional (dë rek′ shən əl)
held together and focused.

excitation mechanism (ek′ sī′ tā′
shən mek′ ə niz′ əm) the part
of the laser that gives it energy.

feedback mechanism (fēd′
bak′ mek′ ə niz′ əm) the
system of mirrors which helps
make the light stronger by
bouncing it back into the active
medium.

monochromatic (mä nō krō mat′
ic) one color.

output coupler (aüt′ püt kəp′
ler) a special mirror made to
allow some of the light to escape
the active medium.

INDEX